WHAT'S NEXT FOR COMMUNICATION?

Tom Jackson

WAYLAND

Published in paperback in 2014 by Wayland
Copyright © Wayland 2014

Wayland
Hachette Children's Books
338 Euston Road
London NW1 3BH

Wayland Australia
Level 17/207 Kent Street
Sydney NSW 2000

Senior editor: Julia Adams
Designer: Maddox Philpot
Illustrator: Maddox Philpot
Consultant: Sean Connolly

Picture acknowledgements:
p. 9 (top): Paul Wicks/Wikipedia;
p. 18 (top): Getty Images; p. 23
(bottom): Mark Williamson/Science
Photo Library; p. 29 (bottom):
Armen Gharibyan/Alamy.

Dewey classification: 302.2
ISBN: 978 0 7502 8365 6

Printed in China

10 9 8 7 6 5 4 3 2 1

Wayland is a division of Hachette
Children's Books,
an Hachette UK Company.
www.hachette.co.uk

COMMUICATION SCIENCE NOW

The human is a talkative animal. We use language to exchange ideas, make plans and, most of all, to gossip about each other. Communication technology has allowed us to talk more than ever, and share all kinds of information as text and pictures. If we can be sure of one thing about the future, we'll all still be communicating; it's just the methods that will evolve!

Down a wire

The tele- in telecommunications or telecoms comes from the Greek word for distant, so it means 'communication at a distance'. There were many early telecoms systems, such as beacon fires sending signals across the country from hilltops, war drums, smoke signals and semaphore flags. But the telegraph – this time meaning 'writing at a distance' – was the first invention that could send signals over the horizon – far out of sight, even around the world. Telegraphic signals – telegrams – were transmitted as pulses of electricity sent along a wire. The code used was invented in the 1830s by Samuel Morse, and his dots and dashes are still used today: Morse Code.

TELEPHONE

As telegraph wires tinkled with the sound of important messages, people had the idea of transmitting voices along it too. In 1876, 40 years after the first telegram, the telephone was born. At first you had to ask an operator to connect your call. Then, in the 1920s, telephones were fitted with a round number dial, so you could input the number and get connected automatically. The dial was replaced in the 1980s by a keypad, but we still dial numbers to call someone.

Voice, text, data

By the 1960s, we were sending more than just conversations down telephone wires. Anything — a voice, some text or a picture — was converted into electrical signals and sent through the network. It was not just telephones that had a network; computers could be connected in the same way, and in 1969 when these networks were hooked together into a network of networks, the internet was born. What happened next is the greatest revolution in communication technology the world had seen since we invented printing — the digital revolution. And it is still going on today.

To the future!

In this book we'll look at the latest research and scientific developments and explore how they might change the way we communicate in the years to come. An icon next to each technology we introduce will give you an idea of when they may become a part of our daily lives.

Who's on the line?

It is easy to meet up with old friends and make new ones using today's communication services. However, it is also easy for people to pretend to be someone they are not. Never give out your address or other personal details to strangers online.

JUST TALKING

The word 'telephone' was made up in the 1870s. It means 'distance talker' and that is exactly what telephones are for. Most of us now carry a telephone with us wherever we go, and future developments will mean we can use this small communicator to chat in new ways.

Good morning, friend. How are you today?

Bonjour ami. Comment allez-vous aujourd'hui?

Talking to the world

`20 YEARS`

There is an ancient barrier to communication: different languages. If we are using different words, we can't understand each other. Computer translators can already recognise one language and change it into another. The more we use them, the more they improve their translation skills. In future, these translators will be combined with voice recognition software and added to the telephone network. We can speak as normal into the phone, but at the other end, our words will come out in whatever language the caller wants.

I think, therefore I chat

`30 YEARS`

For a long time, sci-fi stories have imagined people using telepathy: communicating with their minds instead of their voices. As scientists learn how to convert brain waves into electrical signals, a future telephone could have a brain scanner instead of a microphone. This will transmit what you are thinking, rather than what you are saying.

"LOL"

Charging about

10 YEARS

In future, if our phones run out of battery, we can charge them with electricity stored in our clothes. The cotton is treated with chemicals to create several ultrathin layers on the surface that can hold an electrical charge. That makes the cloth a capacitor – a device that stores electricity. When the phone runs low on power, we just plug it into our T-shirt. Of course, when we get home we'll need to recharge our phone and our clothes ready for the next day!

IT'S ELEMENTARY

What is a capacitor?

A capacitor is a very common electrical component. It is made up of a thin electrified sheet, which would normally be metal, but any material that conducts, or carries electricity, would do. The conductor is then coated in an insulator – a substance that blocks electricity from flowing out. Electricity floods into the capacitor, filling it with charge. When the electricity is switched off, the charge stays inside. If the capacitor is connected up to an electric circuit – like the one used to recharge a battery – the charge flows out again.

FOLD-UP PHONE

5 YEARS

Early mobile phones used to be so large that they came with their own shoulder bag. Now they are much handier in size, but still quite fragile. It will not be long before you can scrunch up your phone and stuff it into your pocket. The bending plastic case will be thin enough to be rolled up or folded, and the flexible screens will be made of organic light-emitting diodes which won't break if bent, dropped or trodden on.

PAUSE FOR THOUGHT

At the moment your thoughts are entirely private, and no one knows what they are until you say them or write them down. If a mobile phone 'brain scanner' is invented that can read your thoughts, would you want to use it?

HANGING OUT

The way we spend time with friends is changing. More and more, we hang out online, talking and joking around with pals who could be next door or on the other side of the world. How will technology help us be sociable in future?

EMAIL THE FUTURE

NOW!

Even after you have died, you could still stay in touch with people in the future. During your lifetime, you would have to upload videos or written messages. These would then be kept secret until a certain date or event after your death – such as your brother or sister's next birthday or the birth of a great grandchild. It may sound sad to you now, but whoever receives a message from beyond the grave might be thrilled!

IT'S ELEMENTARY

Global positioning

One of the technologies a phone uses to pinpoint its location is GPS or the Global Positioning System. This relies on a constellation of 32 satellites, which are orbiting Earth. Your phone exchanges signals with these satellites, and is able to work out your exact location from the signals it receives. The signals travel at the speed of light, so they only take a fraction of a second to reach your phone.

Social gatherings

3 YEARS

At the moment, social networking sites allow us to share jokes, pictures and videos with our circle of friends — and we might chat about them online. We can also invite friends to a real-word event, such as a party. In future, that party could take place online as well, with our voices and live videos of everyone sent to all the other guests!

In your dreams

Scientists are getting closer to recording the brain activity that produces vision – they have taped an image from a cat brain already. As well as helping with vision problems, the technology could be used to record our dreams – or at least the visions we see when we are dreaming. Perhaps one day friends will watch each other's dreams, posted online.

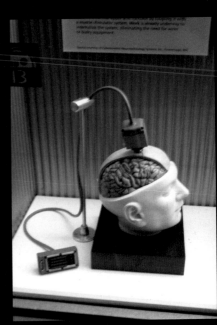

30 YEARS

BrainGate technology uses sensors to interpret brain signals that produce movement. A similar technology could be used to 'read' people's dreams.

People search

2 YEARS

Mobile phones can be used as a tracking device. The phone can calculate its position in a number of ways, which is how it already knows where you are on a map. By sharing that location data with your friends, you will always be able to find each other in a crowd.

PAUSE FOR THOUGHT

Would it be a good thing for us to see where everyone we know is all the time? How would you feel if the location signal from one of your friends was turned off? Would you be tempted to turn off your signal if your family and friends could always see where you were?

SEEING THINGS

They say that a picture speaks a thousand words. It means a picture captures a scene better than any written description. However, one day soon a photograph may actually speak to you. What else can we expect to see in the future?

Curved camera

5 YEARS

The human eye is a light detector, just like the inside of a camera. However, instead of a camera's flat detector, our eyes use a curved layer of light sensors called the retina. The sharpest vision is produced by the fovea — a zone located at the centre of the retina, where the light is most intense. The latest cameras use curved detectors to see like an eye. They create 'foveal' photos and videos, where the centre of the image is very sharp, while the surroundings are less focused.

Saying "cheese"

3 YEARS

Not only will saying "cheese" make everyone smile, it will also take the photo. Future cameras will learn to detect your voice and take a photo whenever you say a code word.

Smellographs

10 YEARS

Printing a photograph involves spraying dots of coloured chemicals onto a piece of paper. Together they make up the whole image. As well as colourful chemicals, we will also be able to add smelly ones which recreate the scent of the image.

Video tattoo

20 YEARS

Ultrafine flexible electronics will allow you to turn your skin into a screen. The temporary layer could be used for something quite normal like reading text messages or watching video clips. However, perhaps people will use them like clothes and makeup, to display moving patterns on their skin that they can change to suit their clothes, or light up in time to music.

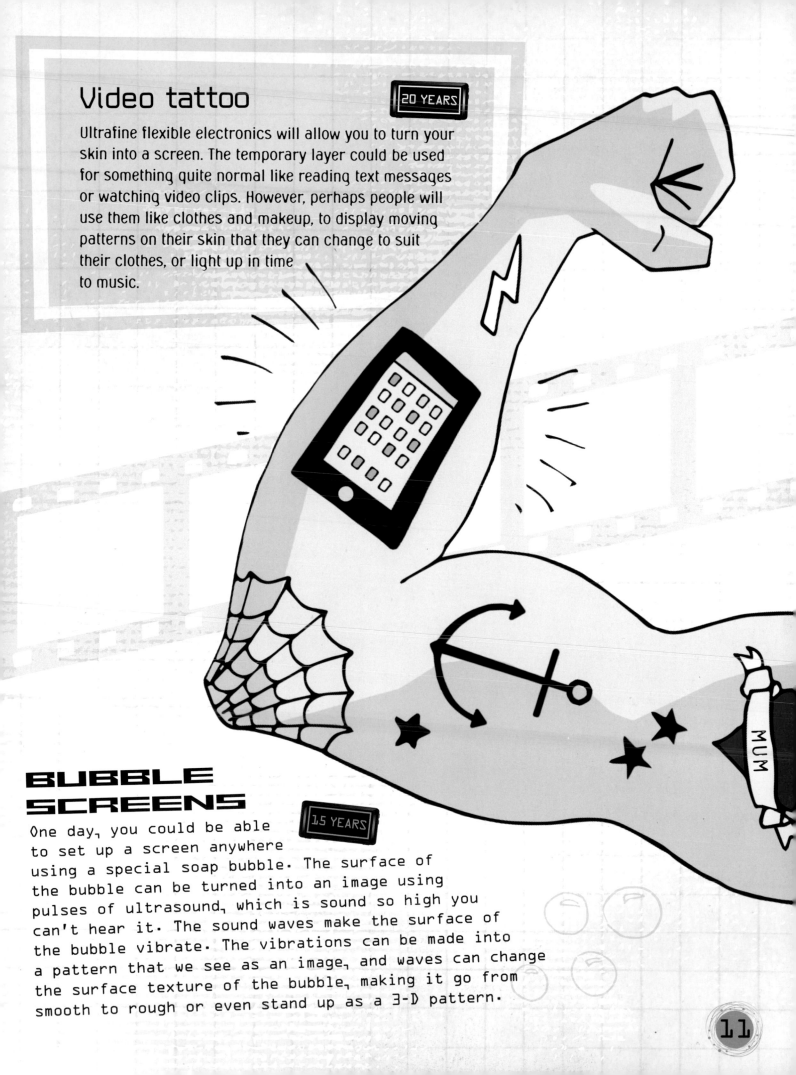

BUBBLE SCREENS

15 YEARS

One day, you could be able to set up a screen anywhere using a special soap bubble. The surface of the bubble can be turned into an image using pulses of ultrasound, which is sound so high you can't hear it. The sound waves make the surface of the bubble vibrate. The vibrations can be made into a pattern that we see as an image, and waves can change the surface texture of the bubble, making it go from smooth to rough or even stand up as a 3-D pattern.

TAKING CONTROL

Being able to communicate easily is not just about having large, powerful networks that connect our computers and phones. Our communication devices need to be easy to use. Let's take a look at how we will interact with machines in future.

Window screen

5 YEARS

When is a window not a window? When it is a screen! Most rooms have a window to see outside, but in future a window will also be a solar-powered computer touchscreen. As you admire the view, you can also read the news or check the weather. If you want to dim the light levels to watch a film, instead of drawing curtains over the window, its glass will just go dark, blocking out the view from inside and out.

Under the skin

10 YEARS

Research has shown that buttons and lights all work fine even when they are embedded under the skin. They can send and receive signals via radio waves. So far this technology has only been tested under dead people's skin, but in future we may choose to have all kinds of gadgets implanted into us – from alarm clocks and remote controls to mobile phones.

Scratch and pinch

5 YEARS

In future, interfaces will get more sensitive to our touch. They will be able to tell the difference between a swipe with a fingertip, a flick with a fingernail and a knock with a knuckle. Adding more of these control 'gestures' allows us to do complicated tasks with just one hand.

Electronic paper

We can look at the news on screens today, but many people still like reading it off paper. Imagine opening a newspaper and seeing the trailer for the latest film and then reading a review; or watching a speech by a politician before reading what everyone thought about it. This could be how we read news in future: with flexible electronic screens printed onto paper, where today there are just photographs.

20 YEARS

Mighty morphing touchscreen

There is no need for a keyboard when you have a touchscreen. Any buttons or keys appear when they are needed. However, it is quite easy to miss them and press the wrong one. In future, touchscreens will be able to change shape, with easy-to-press buttons bulging out of the surface and then flattening again when not required.

10 YEARS

IT'S ELEMENTARY

How can a touchscreen 'feel'?

There are several ways a touchscreen can pick up a finger swipe or tap. A mobile phone screen has a see-through layer on the front of the screen that is electrically charged. When you push gently, your finger changes the amount of charge stored in that region of the screen. Heavy-duty touchscreens like those at a railway station or in a museum work by a finger pushing two electrified layers together.

13

BEING THERE

Despite it being easier, cheaper and faster than ever to send and receive messages, or chat over video links, people still say there is nothing like talking face-to-face. However, in future there might be another way. Experts call it telepresence; it uses technology that allows you to be in two places at once.

By remote control

15 YEARS

It is easy enough to imagine being able to hear and see everything coming from cameras and microphones on a robot who is somewhere else in the world. In the future, clever gloves and body suits will also help you 'feel' what the robot touches. You will be able to control the robot's movements with your thoughts while you are on the other side of the globe! In 2012, researchers managed to use a brain scanner to pick up commands from the brain and transmit them to a robot.

PAUSE FOR THOUGHT

If you are steering a remote-control robot and someone hits the machine, is it the same as them hitting you or is it not so bad? How should a remote-control robot get treated — like the human controlling it?

LONG-DISTANCE KISS

Blowing a kiss is a nice touch, but not as nice as the real thing. One day you might be able to send and receive a kiss through the internet. A device called Kissenger, invented in 2012, has a pair of pressure-sensitive plastic lips. When you kiss them, they change shape a little, and this information is sent to another Kissenger belonging to your sweetheart. The lips on this second device recreate the exact shape of your own lips and kiss your partner on your behalf.

AS IF YOU WERE THERE...

5 YEARS

In recent years, superstars have been appearing on stage as holograms. The audiences see what looks like their hero on stage — even if the performer in question died some time ago. The technology uses an old theatre trick to project the video of the performer onto an angled see-through screen. The rest of the stage is lit in such as way that the hologram appears among dancers or in front of scenery. This same technique could be converted to transmit a live video of a person into an important meeting, to give a lecture, or to make a speech at a wedding.

ROBOT ASSISTANT

20 YEARS

Oh, to be in two places (or even more) at once - just imagine what you could do! The latest artificial intelligence research is trying to turn robots into helpful assistants. The robots are learning how to recognise where they are by identifying what is around them; for example, bathrooms have toilets, car parks have cars in rows, and real parks have grass, trees and swings. Such a robot could be asked to help whenever you are not there – such as posting an important letter or emptying the dishwasher when it's your turn.

SEARCH

The internet's great advantage is that anyone can add information to it. But then we hit a problem: how does anyone know what is available, and where do we find the stuff that we want among all the stuff we don't? The invention of the internet led to a new invention: the search engine. And like the internet, search services are constantly developing.

Preference engine

Search engines work by rating web sites. The rating reflects how closely it matches the search words you've used, but it also rates sites according to how many other people have used that same page for the same reasons — the more people have used a site, the more relevant it must be. However, in future, search engines will also begin to take your personal preferences into account. Your history of internet use will give the search engine an idea of what you like and what you don't and so it can rate results to suit you more exactly.

5 YEARS

STACKS OF FACTS

The search engine Google is named after the googol, a large number that consists of a one with 100 zeros.

One of the first web search engines was called Veronica, which stood for Very Easy Rodent-Oriented Net-wide Index to Computerized Archives. The rodent in question was Gopher, the name of the system used to share files on the early web.

Search engines have to constantly survey the web to find out what is being added and taken down. They do this automatically with programs called web crawlers.

Extra memory

20 YEARS

In the days before the web and communications technology, people's memories were filled with important things, like telephone numbers and addresses. Now we store all that information on computers and can retrieve them with a few touches of a button. If there is anything we don't know, we just 'google' it. In future, we might be able to link our memories to a search engine — if we can't recall a fact from memory, we will automatically get it from the web.

Crowdsourcing

There is a phenomenon called 'the wisdom of crowds'. It suggests that a single guess or estimate is very unlikely to give an accurate answer to a question, but the average of hundreds of different estimates is more likely to be very close to the exact answer. Solving problems in this way is called crowdsourcing, where large numbers of answers are collected using the internet and averaged out. The internet lets us gather lots of opinions quickly, so in future we will gather all kinds of information by crowdsourcing: governments will figure out the best new laws; fashion designers will find cool trends; and journalists will seek out the latest stories.

PICTURE SEARCH

NOW!

Have you ever wanted to know more about an amazing building you've seen on holiday or the name of a strange animal? Instead of searching the internet about it using words, you could just take a photo of it and search that way. For this kind of search to work, the search engine guesses at what is in the picture, based on its shapes and colours. As more images are submitted, the guesses will become more accurate.

MAKING CONNECTIONS

While we chat on the phone or send a text message, it is easy to forget that we are sending a signal down a lot of wires and cables and through a lot of computers. In future, this technology behind the scenes will get even faster and more efficient.

Nanochips

20 YEARS

Although they sound small, there is a limit to how small microchips can get. While we can shrink them down to a certain degree, we need a different technology to go beyond a certain size. The solution is the nanochip. The components on a microchip are cut into the surface. But on a nanochip they are built one atom at a time using a very fine tool called a nanoprobe, which can push atoms into precise shapes. The components on a nanochip are thousands of times smaller than today's microchips, and all those extra components will allow computers to run thousands of times faster.

This is a nano-bible, created using nano technology: the entire bible is printed onto a gold-plated silicon chip that is 0.5 mm squared.

YOGHURT COMPUTER

A tub of yoghurt will not just be a tasty treat in future – it might also be also used to make electronics. Yoghurt is a mass of bacteria living in milk. The bacteria can grow very quickly, and we could harness these hard-working bugs to build nano-sized devices (that means we measure them in billionths of a metre!). Instead of milk, the specially engineered yoghurt would be fed magnetic iron particles, which the bacteria would build into tiny high-tech components.

50 YEARS

IT'S ELEMENTARY

SILICON CHIPS

Silicon chips, or microchips, contain millions of minute electronic components, which work like switches and gates that direct electric currents this way and that. They are called silicon chips because that is what they are made of – a sliver of pure silicon; the components are etched on to the surface.

Twisted light

15 YEARS

Optical fibres carry coded information as flashes of light. The light beams bounce along inside the fibre at the speed of light. One fibre can carry 160 separate beams, each one sent as a unique colour. However, researchers think they can almost double the amount of information transferred via optical fibres, which would be enough to fill 60 DVDs every second. That would be achieved by making the light beams twist into spirals as they travel. Each signal would have a unique number of turns that could be used to tell them apart.

Brain computer

40 YEARS

A computer can only work as fast as its processor, which is the bit that runs the programs and coordinates the computer's activities. The fastest supercomputers have dozens of processors all working together, and they can handle 1,000 trillion commands in a second. Future computers will have millions of tiny processors – more like the human brain. However, all that activity will make a lot of heat and so some suggest computers will need to be filled with a cooling gel, and the processors will connect to each other, not using electricity, but by flickering light signals.

⚠ ERROR ALERT

Photophone

The first wireless mobile phone was invented in 1880 by Alexander Graham Bell. (He'd already invented the regular telephone.) Bell's device was called a photophone because it sent signals as a beam of light. It worked — just about — but although Bell was way ahead of his time, within a few years wireless technology was using radio waves instead, which it still does today and has proven to be far more reliable over long distances.

SHOPPING

Even over the last few years, the way we shop has changed a lot. No longer do we pop to the high street or megastore to purchase what we need – we just go online and click on what we are after. Communications technology is going to keep giving us faster and better ways to shop.

Virtual shopper

5 YEARS

Everyone likes a bargain, and in future, shops will be able to make you an offer you can't refuse. An app on your mobile phone will alert the store that you are passing nearby and send it your wish list – the items you have been thinking about buying. If the store stocks one of the products, it will send a voucher to your phone, offering a special deal if you come in and buy it right now. The app will also have access to you bank account, so it only sends out requests for wish-list items that you can afford there and then – and warns you if you are overspending.

PAUSE FOR THOUGHT

Do you think it's a good idea for stores to know your likes, dislikes and needs, as well as how much money you have?

Digital wallets

2 YEARS

One day coins, bank notes and credit cards will disappear. That does not mean we'll stop using money, it will just all be stored in a digital wallet on your smartphone or computer. To pay for shopping, your phone connects to the checkout using close-range radio signals. Once linked, there is a security check before money is moved from your bank account to the shop's. You'll even use the system to send money to friends and relatives by text message.

LIFE-SIZE LOOK

5 YEARS

One problem with shopping online is that you can't touch a product before you buy it. It can be a surprise when the item is delivered and it is much smaller – or bigger – than you needed. Soon shopping sites will detect the size of the screen you are using and display items at actual life-size.

FRIDGE SCANNER

10 YEARS

The supermarket already uses lasers and weighing scales to find out what food you have in your basket. One day your fridge and freezer at home will use the same technology. For example, as you put an item in the freezer, a laser will scan the barcode and the freezer know it is your favourite ice cream (an essential item!). The shelves have touch sensors, so the fridge and freezer always know where everything is. When one item is nearly used up (they can tell by its weight) they add it to the shopping list, or even order a replacement automatically.

HELPING OUT

New technology is all about doing things better and making life easier. Here are a few ways communication technology of the future will give us a helping hand.

GETTING SOME GUIDANCE

10 YEARS

Imagine you are an engineer or mechanic, and it is your job to mend engines, heating systems or network connections. Every job is different from the last and it can take a while to figure out what you are working with. In future this could be a lot easier. Simply zap a barcode or punch in a serial number, and you will immediately receive the plans from the manufacturer. These plans will be displayed on a headset, so you can take a look at them while your hands are free to go to work.

3-D printers

10 YEARS

An inkjet printer recreates text and pictures by squirting drops of quick-drying ink onto paper. The same printing system can use other chemicals, not just ink. For example, a printer can use liquid plastic that hardens when it meets air. It takes longer than printing a photo, but a printer can create a 3-D object, building it up in layers. You can download the designs for everything from a lunchbox to a fake flower; then just press print! You can even print the components for a new 3-D printer.

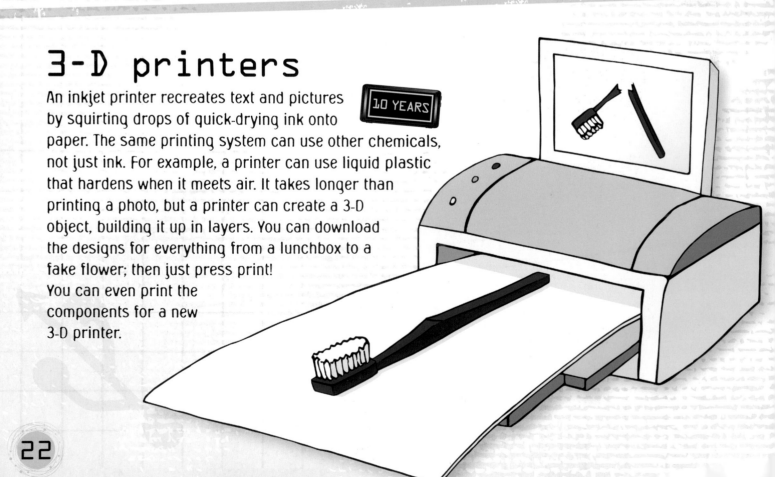

LOST AND FOUND

20 YEARS

In a connected world, every object from a toy to a thermometer will have some kind of identification signal.
We will be able to make use of that to locate lost items. We'll just have to look around the room using the camera of our phone or tablet to see where the item is. If it's in a cupboard, it will show up on the screen as being inside – almost like X-ray vision!

Healing plastic

15 YEARS

Our hand-held devices are pretty sturdy and normally keep working even if the outer casing gets cracked in an accident. In future, you might not even need to replace the case. Self-healing plastics will mend themselves; cracked sections go red and re-form when exposed to sunlight.

Microsatellites, such as this one, measuring 10 cm on each side, are already being used in scientific research today.

Personal spacecraft

20 YEARS

OK, they'll be way too small to fly in, but soon we will be able to launch our own picosatellites. They weigh just a few hundred grammes — similar to a mobile phone. It will still cost a few hundred pounds to get them into space, but once they get there, you are in charge. Why do you need your own satellite? Well, it could provide your very own satellite link to people in remote places, or give you a personal tour of Earth from space.

OUT AT WORK

'Going to work' will mean many things in future. Cloud computing, where everyone uses a little bit of a vast global network of computing services, will mean people will be able to work anywhere in the world.

Sharing work

Computers are good at moving files – we can **20 YEARS** send them between workstations using email or a file sharing system. In future, this will be even easier. A file displayed on a screen could be 'swept' onto your tablet computer with a wave of the hand. Alternatively, you could take a photo of the file icon with your device, and the file itself would be automatically transferred.

STACKS OF FACTS

The Cloud is actually a farm, or a series of farms. All the computers that store our data are called servers; thousands of them are stored at server farms.

Microsoft has around half a million servers on its farms.

It can get hot in a server farm with all those high-speed computers. The most efficient farms are in cold places, such as Scandinavia and Iceland.

Rank and file

You can use the internet to search for webpages, but also for people. This is very useful for finding experts for a particular job. In future, 'people search' results will rate everyone according to their qualifications, skills, location and whether other people think they do a good job.

5 YEARS

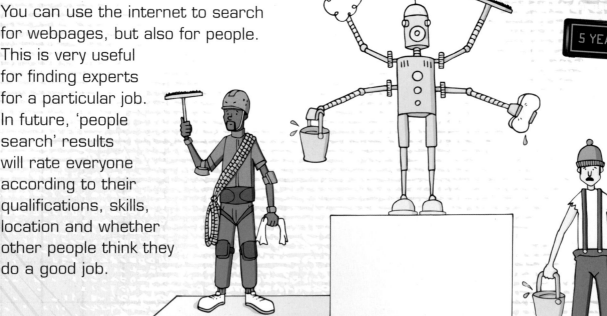

Rent a computer

10 YEARS

Cloud computing will do away with much of the computer hardware we use today. You could make do with just a fold-up screen and keyboard. All your work and personal records are stored 'on the Cloud' and you access them through wireless connections in cafés, at school – or even in parks. If you wanted an application – a word processor, perhaps – you could rent it from the cloud, and it would work just as well as if it were installed on your own computer.

Cyber money

NOW!

Computers can make money – literally. Bitcoin is an online currency that started in 2009. Each Bitcoin is 'mined' by the user of a powerful computer solving a complicated maths puzzle. Miners then pay for things online using the Bitcoins they have earned. As more and more Bitcoins are mined, the maths puzzles get more complicated. That stops too many Bitcoins being produced too quickly – if lots of people have lots of Bitcoins, they are not worth as much.

SECURITY

Advances in communication will make life easier and more fun, but we will all have to be careful about who we communicate with – and whether anyone else is listening in. Common sense will help us stay safe, but security systems will also be very important.

ID parade

5 YEARS

In an online world where it is easy to pretend to be someone else, it will become more and more important to prove exactly who we are. The best way to identify ourselves is to use our own body. It is unique to you and you can't lose it or leave it at home by mistake like an ID card. Biometric ID systems measure body features, such as the iris or fingerprint, a voice or even the smell of the skin.

SNIFFING OUT INFORMATION

NOW!

There is a lot of information on the internet if you know where to look. Banks use software called algo-sniffers. These sift through the financial activity of rival banks to see if they can quickly spot an algorithm – a computer-formula that might be used to manage the buying and selling of shares. The information on such algorithms is very useful to competitors. As a result, all banks guard against algo-sniffers by deploying further software: algo-sniffer-sniffers!

PAUSE FOR THOUGHT

Facial recognition systems can spot a face in a crowd. Police use facial recognition to find wanted criminals among videos of people walking around towns. How do you feel about computers checking and recognising your face at any given time?

26

QUANTUM CODES

Important information is sent in code, so that if it falls into the wrong hands, its secrets stay hidden. Every code has a key, the way of revealing the hidden message. This is the only thing that has to be sent in absolute secrecy. The best way to do this is using a quantum code. The key is sent as a single photon of light, which has a specific set of characteristics – such as the way the photon spins. These features can only be observed once. Afterwards the photon will display a different set of characteristics. If a spy intercepts the key as it is being sent, the key will be changed – and can never be used.

20 YEARS

Alice

Quantum code key

Bob

If someone intercepts when Alice is sending a quantum code key to Bob, the key immediately changes its characteristics and cannot be used.

Cyber attacks are launched using botnets: huge networks of hijacked computers called zombies. A computer becomes a zombie when a virus allows someone else to secretly take control of it.

STACKS OF FACTS

Titan Rain was a cyber attack that lasted for three years. It started in 2003 and involved secrets being stolen from the computers at American weapons and aircraft manufacturers. No one is sure who was behind it.

WEARING TECHNOLOGY

The history of communication has shown that our gadgets keep getting smarter. The latest smartphone is a camera, computer, games machine, torch, scanner – and telephone – all rolled into one. However, perhaps one day using a smartphone will seem very old-fashioned. The next big step in communication will be wearable devices.

Wearing a screen

5 YEARS

Perhaps mobile phones will be replaced with a pair of glasses, which function as a camera, telephone, mobile computer and screen all at once. The gadget will be controlled by voice commands. For example, if you ask it "Where is the bus station?" it will guide you there by displaying arrows on the eyepiece screen. Meanwhile you get a text message: "UR L8. You missed the bus." You then say "I need a taxi!" and the inbuilt telephone dials the nearest taxi company. And of course, if you are short-sighted, this headset will also work like a pair of glasses.

Smaller, better

Of course the glasses described here will probably become out of date and made even smaller. Perhaps all we will need in its place is a single, very smart, contact lens on one eye.

LAYERS

NOW!

Looking through web-enabled glasses makes it easier to merge the real world with information from the internet. The approach is called augmented reality (AR) – augmented means 'made better'. As you look around, you will see information on the things you see displayed as an AR layer. The layer might show where the cafés are in the area. As you swing your head, you will see icons pinpointing the direction of each one. The layer includes perspective, too. The nearer cafés will appear as a larger icons than the ones further away.

LIFE IN REPLAY

5 YEARS

Web-enabled glasses will be able to record the sights and sounds of your day, and you can replay the best bits later. That might change the way we observe the world – if it is all being recorded we don't need to pay so much attention in the moment. We can always look at the recording later.

PAUSE FOR THOUGHT

Is recording your life always a good thing? When will you have time to watch it back?

Flexible charger

10 YEARS

You may carry a hand-held projector that shines a keyboard onto a flat surface using a strong light. You might have the latest gadget-packed eyewear. Whichever device you carry, they will all need power. You could wear the solar panels that charge them up. Flexible panels could be sewn into your hat, coat and even your bag.

Flexible solar panels on a bag could also power a light, so you can see your bag's contents!

GLOSSARY

3-D Short for three-dimensional; when a flat picture on a screen (or even paper) is presented in such a way that it looks like it is a real object, with length and width as well as depth.

algorithm A list of instructions – normally mathematical ones – for performing a task; computer programs are a series of interconnected algorithms.

artificial Made by people; the opposite of natural.

augmented reality When ordinary reality, such as the view around us or the pages of a book or magazine, are added to (or augmented) by content from a computer.

average The middle amount.

conductor A material that carries, or conducts, electricity; see insulator.

constellation A collection of objects in the sky, such as stars or a group of satellites.

cyber To do with computers.

fovea The most sensitive part of the human eye, where very sharp detailed images are formed.

gestures The ways we control a computer or other device by touching a screen or moving our hands or other body parts.

hologram A 3-D image.

inflate To blow up with air.

inkjet A type of printer where the ink, or other liquid, is squirted through tiny holes to create patterns of minute dots.

insulator A material that does not carry an electric current, stopping it from passing.

morph To change shape.

nano- To do with tiny objects that are measured in billionths of metres.

network A group of computers that are connected together, so they can share information and work together.

phenomenon   Something that has been observed to occur in nature.

photon   A particle that carries light.

quantum   A fixed, unchanging quantity; quantum physics studies how packets of energy make up the universe.

retina   The light-sensitive layer at the back of the eye.

rodent   A small animal that gnaws its food, such as a mouse, rat, or gopher.

software   The programs and applications that make a computer work; the hardware refers to microchips, screens and keyboards.

technology   Using scientific knowledge to make useful tools.

telecommunications   To communicate over long distances.

telepathy   To communicate by thinking messages, rather than writing or saying them.

ultra-   A term that means 'extremely'.

ultrasound   Sound that is extremely high-pitched, far too high for humans to hear.

USEFUL WEBSITES:

This website takes a look at what is happening right now — communication technology connects us to each other like never before:
http://now.sprint.com/nownetwork/

Microsoft led the personal computer revolution in the 1980s. This is what they think the world will be like in the years ahead:
http://www.youtube.com/watch?v=cYCez_DoHpo

Take a look out of the window — a smart window that is! One day we might all see the world this way:
https://www.youtube.com/watch?v=mTVPVobDrms

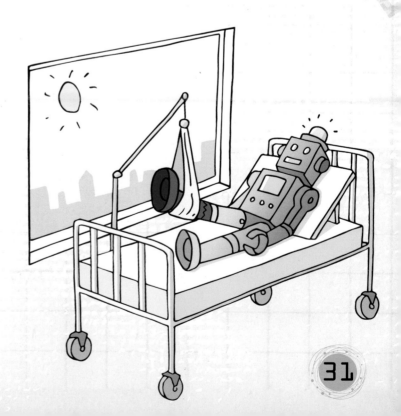

INDEX